The book of A[...] [...]ve
relationship in [...] ns
fills out this pictu[...] [...]y[...]

DARRELL BOCK,
Senior Research Professor of New Testament,
Dallas Theological Seminary, Dallas, Texas
and author of *Acts*, Baker Exegetical Commentary

Many people build their lives on a weak foundation
of sand. In *Foundations*, Peter Mead introduces you
to the one concrete foundation poured deep enough
to hold your life steady!

TONY REINKE,
Writer for Desiring God Ministries, Minneapolis, Minnesota
and author of *Lit!*

Peter's love of scripture, and his desire to see lives
transformed bleed through the pages of this book.
Explore the foundations of Christianity and engage
anew the true story of a relationship between a
human race whose sin is greater than we think, and
a God whose grace is more amazing than we could
imagine!

RICK MCKINLEY,
Leader Pastor of Imago Dei Community, Portland, Oregon.

A great little primer about the world, ourselves and
– most importantly – God. This short, easy to read,
helpful book will help you get to know Him better.

MARCUS HONEYSETT,
Director of Living Leadership, Kent, England

Having the right answers is one thing but Peter Mead '
goes deeper – he explores the right questions –

questions of God, humanity, sin and salvation. By turning to Scripture this book gives us a surprising, satisfying and compelling foundation for life.

GLEN SCRIVENER,
Evangelist, Speak Life

Peter Mead provides the important foundational questions – and answers – that people should be raising when it comes to faith in Christ. This concise book is just what is needed to build belief and believers!

SCOTT M. GIBSON,
Haddon W. Robinson Professor of Preaching,
Gordon-Conwell Theological Seminary,
South Hamilton, Massachusetts.

FOUNDATIONS

FOUR BIG QUESTIONS WE SHOULD BE ASKING BUT TYPICALLY DON'T

PETER MEAD

CHRISTIAN
FOCUS

Copyright ° Peter Mead 2015

paperback ISBN 978-1-78191-641-4
epub ISBN 978-1-78191-686-5
mobi ISBN 978-1-78191-687-2

10 9 8 7 6 5 4 3 2 1

Published in 2015
by
Christian Focus Publications,
Geanies House, Fearn,
Ross-shire, IV20 1TW, Scotland
www.christianfocus.com

Cover design by Daniel van Straaten
Printed by Nørhaven, Denmark

Contents

Foreword *by Tim Chester* 7

Introduction..11

Part 1: The Four Questions...................................15

1. Which god is God?.......................................17

2. What is a Human?..27

3. What is Sin?..41

4. What is Salvation? 57

Part 2: Building on the Four Questions 71

5. Christian Life & Growth...............................73

6. The Four Questions Applied.......................81

Foreword

Which god is God?

What is a human?

What is sin?

What is salvation?

You may never have thought much about these questions. But the fact is we all have a working version of the answers. As we muddle through life, we do so on the basis of some ultimate allegiance (which god is God?). We have some sense of who we are or what we'd like to be (what is a human?). We have some understanding of what's wrong with the world (what is sin?) and how it can be put right (what is salvation?). Our answers to these questions shape our lives. So it makes sense to give some time to thinking about these issues more explicitly. Nothing matters more than getting them right. But where to start?

Instead of speculating about who God is, Peter Mead invites us to begin with the claim that God has revealed Himself in Jesus. What kind of a God emerges from that claim? What kind of a vision for human beings and human flourishing? Christians have a word for it – 'gospel'. It means 'good news'. We think that what emerges is good news – *the* good news.

Christians have a radical view of our problem. But we have an equally radical view of the solution. Other religions and worldviews offer some way by which human beings can solve their own problems. Christians believe our situation is helpless and hopeless. We're enslaved by our selfish desires and estranged from God. But we also believe God Himself has come to rescue us. So our confidence is not in our efforts or achievement. Our confidence is in God's love. Our negative assessment of our problem leads to the most positive sense of joy and hope. *Foundations* is an invitation to explore that hope.

You may not be a Christian. And you may not like the answers proposed in this book. You may not be convinced. But it's worth exploring. It's worth giving it a go. You've got nothing to lose – except an hour or so of your time – and possibly everything to gain.

Or you may be a Christian. Perhaps you take the answers for granted. But Mead invites us to push beyond our assumptions and discover a deeper, richer reality. He suggests we start with the triune God. And if the answer to the god-question is Father, Son and Holy Spirit, then everything else changes.

Tim Chester,
*Pastor of Grace Church, Boroughbridge,
and Curriculum Director
of the Acts 29-Oak Hill Academy.*

Introduction

I am no builder, but I know that foundations are very important. Think about the freestanding cathedral bell tower in Pisa, Italy. Work began in 1173. Five years later the second floor was being built, but the tower had begun to sink on one side. A century later, when work resumed, the engineers tried to compensate for the tilt by building one side of the upper floors taller than the other. While the Leaning Tower of Pisa may be a popular tourist attraction, it is a stark example of the dangers of an inadequate foundation.

Times change. Not only with regard to architecture, but in all areas. The culture my parents grew up in just after the war was very different to the culture my children are growing up in now. For one thing, our culture is so much less aware of biblical content and teaching. But does this mean there is less belief today than there was sixty or seventy years ago?

Not at all. There may well be less belief in the Bible, but there is still belief in something. People may not be believers in God or believers in Jesus, but all human beings are believers. We all believe constantly. All the decisions we make are based on beliefs: we believe a chair will hold our weight and so we sit on it. We believe certain sources of information are trustworthy, while others are to be taken with a pinch of salt. We have beliefs based on past experiences, based on guesswork, based on education, and so on.

This book is about beliefs. Specifically, it is about the foundations of your belief system. Whether you would call yourself a Christian or not, there is a foundation underneath your beliefs. I am convinced if you dig down below everything else, there are four great building blocks underneath any belief system. These great foundation stones are four basic questions. Our personal answers to these questions will determine how we live our lives, how we make choices, as well as what our eternities will look like. Everything is built on our understanding of these four questions. They are:-

Which god is God?

What does it mean to be human?

What is sin?

What is salvation?

This book seeks to answer these questions biblically, focusing on the book of Acts where we can read about the gospel spreading in the early years after Jesus had been on Earth.

Typically, we assume that if someone agrees on the so-called primary issues – is the Bible inspired, is Jesus God, are we saved by grace through faith alone, etc. – then we must be on the same page. Sure, there may be different views on secondary issues (timing of Christ's return, timing and mode of creation), and on tertiary issues (which style of music our church prefers, etc.), but we assume that unity on the primary issues makes for unity between Christians. But what if Christians agreed on all of these things, primary, secondary and tertiary, but disagreed on the four foundational questions? You would end up with a very different Christianity, a very different Gospel and quite possibly an entirely different religion. No amount of compensation at the upper levels of a belief system will truly overcome a failure at the level of the foundation.

If you are intrigued by Christianity, I hope that this little book can be helpful to you. It will not answer everything, but I hope it will point you toward the right questions to be asking. I also hope it will prompt you to pick up a Bible and chase after the God who reveals Himself in those pages.

If you would call yourself a Christian, I hope this little book can be helpful to you. I am convinced the church would be a much healthier community if people actively investigated the questions raised here.

How healthy is the foundation of your belief system? We have to probe the foundational four questions. So let's start with the first one.

Part 1

The
Four
Questions

1: Which god is God?

The first and most important question is the God question. Which god is God? What is He like? How do we know? This is the first foundation stone.

When I speak to someone about spiritual things, I tend to be encouraged when they say that they believe in God.

Which God don't you believe in?

Not so fast! Which God do they believe in? The identity and nature of God determine everything else, so getting these right is critical.

What if someone says they don't believe in God? Then I should probably ask the same follow-up question: which god don't you believe in? This tends to be very revealing, and typically I find I don't believe in that god either! Let's think about the God who reveals Himself in the Bible.

For the purposes of our journey through these four questions, I'd like to point us to the book of Acts. This is the account of the early church as the message of Christianity spread across the Roman Empire from its Jewish beginnings. For the first few chapters it really is all Jerusalem-centred and the church is an entirely Jewish thing.

Then God does two things. First, in chapter 9, He grabs hold of a Jewish anti-Jesus persecutor of the church named Saul of Tarsus (we use his Roman name, Paul). God turns his life upside-down and commissions him to preach about Jesus to the nations. Second, in chapter 10, He convinces Jewish church leader Peter that the message of Jesus is for Gentiles (non-Jews) too.

So in chapter 13 we see Paul heading out from his church to preach the message of Christianity to people in other lands. Interestingly, he always seems to start in a synagogue, preaching to Bible-trained Jews and interested Gentiles. Typically he gets a response from some, but then a jealous backlash from others, resulting in his having to leave the synagogue, and often the town too.

But there are two occasions where Paul preaches to an entirely pagan crowd, a group of people who had no Bible awareness, no Bible stories as children and no Bible training as adults. What does Paul say to these people? Interestingly, he makes answering the God question his top priority.

CHURNING THINGS UP IN LYSTRA
(ACTS 14:8-20)

In Lystra we see the healing of a crippled man creating a big stir and leading to an opportunity to preach the Gospel. Barnabas and Paul find themselves being identified as the Greek god Zeus, with his communications director, Hermes. Things get even more awkward when the priests of Zeus show up with a bull to sacrifice to them! So what do they do? Do they affirm the people's belief in a powerful god-figure and go on to explain the elements that were slightly off target? Not at all! They resist the whole scenario and declare that this sacrifice must not occur. Then Luke records a mini-sermon synopsis for us:

> 'Men, why are you doing these things? We also are men, of like nature with you, and we bring you good news, that you should turn from these vain things to a living God, who made the heaven and the earth and the sea and all that is in them. In past generations he allowed all the nations to walk in their own ways. Yet he did not leave himself without witness, for he did good by giving you rains from heaven and fruitful seasons, satisfying your hearts with food and gladness'(Acts 14:15-17)

The whole message is offering an initial answer to the *Which God?* question. Paul urges them to turn from these vain things to the living God. He is the patient God, the kind God, the God who is the creator, the life-giver, the generous God... that one!

CREATING TENSIONS IN ATHENS
(ACTS 17:16-34)

Just a few chapters later we find Paul on his second missionary journey, this time arriving in Europe and coming alone to Athens. While he waits for his colleagues to catch up he wanders around and sees the idols placed all over the area. He finds the culture distressing, but then gets an opportunity to speak before the gathered philosophers at the Areopagus. Does he accept their religious awareness and then seek merely to add and tweak? No, again he presents the real God from scratch.

> 'Men of Athens, I perceive that in every way you are very religious. For as I passed along and observed the objects of your worship, I found also an altar with this inscription, "To the unknown god." What therefore you worship as unknown, this I proclaim to you. The God who made the world and everything in it, ... being Lord of heaven and earth ... gives to all mankind life and breath and

everything...that they should seek God, and
perhaps feel their way toward him and find
him..' (Acts 17:22-27)

His message feels a lot like the synopsis we saw
from Lystra: God is the life-giving, in charge, generous, kind, wanting-to-be-known God. Their
approach to divine things is ignorant, but Paul
invites them to reject false gods and turn to the
true and living God. The resurrection of Jesus is
the proof of the coming judgment that will end
this window of opportunity. At this point Paul
seems to have been interrupted, but there were
a few who believed.

There are at least three things we should
learn from Paul as he spoke of God in these two
passages.

1. Paul did not bypass the *Which God?* question. On both occasions where the audience did
not know their Bibles, Paul answered this question as the first priority. It is dangerous to assume
that people know what is meant by the term
'God.'

2. Paul had one source of information about
this God. In Athens he was speaking to a mixed
group of both Epicurean and Stoic philosophers.
That sounds intimidating. Actually, we are all
effectively amateur philosophers: we try to make
sense of the world based on the information we

have and our own common sense. Similarly, all philosophers are theologians because they are trying to make sense of everything, including any ultimate divine being.

Stoics had a certain view of God; they saw the divine being as the pre-determiner. They believed that we live in a world where we need to engage our minds and think clearly, not letting our dangerous emotions carry us anywhere, and we need to be self-sufficient, rational and efficient. (To illustrate this with a slightly unfair caricature, this is a bit like the common view of the older generation's approach to life: the stiff-upper-lip approach.)

Epicureans also had their own view of God. They also saw the divine being as distant and impersonal. Their mantra was something like, 'there is nothing to fear in God and nothing to fear in death, so just attain good and endure evil.' The result was a live-it-up mentality. Go for the thrill. Live in the moment. If it feels good, just do it. (To give another unfair caricature, this is how many today would typically view the younger generation.)

Many have observed that Paul never quotes from the Bible, while he does quote from their own poets. In fact, he is brilliantly on target, with every line pointed at the Stoics, or the Epicureans, or both. So no Bible quotes, but two poet quotes. However, don't miss a critical point here: the source of his information was not philoso-phy, or culturally defined ideas from poetry. Rather, it was all profoundly bib-lical. Every statement Paul makes shows he had his nose in his Bible a lot!

Paul had his nose in his Bible a lot!

For centuries, people have been bringing philosophical assumptions about God to the Bible and have tried to blend what the Bible says with 'what we know is true of God.' This most often means that they are attempting to blend a distant and unknowable divine 'it' with the God of the Bible who has stepped in and made Himself known (see John 1:18).

All philosophical speculations about God tend to imagine a god who is completely self-absorbed, but the God of the Bible is completely self-giving. The god of philosophical speculation will typically be an enlarged projection of ourselves – a bigger, more impressive me as measured by the values of this world. As a result, speculative views of god always make Him out to be a glory-grabbing self-absorbed being (a bigger version of fallen humanity). By contrast, the God of the Bible is all-glorious, but He gives glory instead of grabbing at it. The God of the Bible and the god of philosophical speculation are very different and we should give up on combining the two, once and for all.

This is not to say that we should not give God all the glory, nor that God will ever share His glory with another god or mini-god (see Isa. 43:7, for instance). All of creation is an overflow of the gloriously loving and self-giving fellowship of the Trinity, so all of creation exists by and for the glory of God. The key issue is the nature of that glory – is it the self-absorbed obsession of an imagined divine being, or the self-giving goodness of the God of the Bible?

Perhaps you have never studied philosophy or tried to write a paper combining the two presentations of God. Here is how we can know if we are doing just that in our thinking. When we assume we can speak of God based on a set of truths before coming to the Bible, we are doing what I am describing. 'We know God is the ultimate Supreme Being and super powerful and everything is for His glory and you can't really know Him…' – these are statements that reveal a composite view of God, even if most of this is true and you can attach Bible verses!

The mistake is that we think we are already somewhere in our knowledge of God. But we need to get into the Bible and know God on His terms. What is God like? He is like Jesus. When Jesus was asked for a glimpse of God the Father in John 14, He replied, 'Who-ever has seen me has seen the Father' (v.9).

What is God like? He is like Jesus.

If we think we can under-stand God based on our own common sense, or a set of ab-stract truths, then we are making a philosophi-cal mistake. Our first principle needs to be that we cannot know God through our own human reason; we need to find out what He says about Himself. Let's chase God in His Word as if it is the most important quest of our lives.

Incidentally, in the Reformation of the sixteenth century, Martin Luther fought vehemently against the place of philosophy in the training of church leaders; he wanted people getting back to their Bibles. The influence of philosophy on the church had been too great. In the same way, we should be people of the Book, letting God show us who He is, instead of assuming we can know some basic truths about Him before we open the Bible.

3. Paul's manner and tone reflected the God he introduced. In Acts 17:16 it says he was distressed, provoked, and angered on the inside

as he saw how the things of God were confused by the culture. We should feel the same as we observe the presentation of Christianity in our media and culture. But notice verses 22-23. When he speaks to the people, Paul's tone is not angry and his manner is not aggressive. 'I perceive that in every way you are very religious.' Nice. He then refers to their statues not as 'demonic idols' but as 'objects of worship.' His tone is respectful, gracious, kind and patient. This is important.

Too many people have been put off Christianity by preachers and people talking of Jesus in an angry, barking tone. Of course we are provoked by the lies propagated in the culture, but everyone who actually knows God personally should represent the love and grace of the God we worship.

So which God is the real God and what is He like? Do we look to our own understanding, or do we look to Jesus? The real God really is good news!

REFLECTION QUESTIONS:

- ❧ What are the first words you would use to describe God?

- ❧ How much of your thinking about God comes from the Bible, and how much is just truth everyone assumes?

2: What is a Human?

What does it mean to be human? This is the second critical question, and it may be one that you have never really pondered.

When Paul was preaching to biblically unaware philosophers in Acts 17, he not only started from scratch and answered the *Which God?* question, but he also spoke about what it means to be human. He never quoted the Bible, but his content was dripping in biblical truth. In fact, the two quotes he gave from the Greek poets, Epimenides and Aratus, were reframed to communicate biblical truth about this second foundational question. Here are the quotes:

> "In him we live and move and have our being," and, "For we are indeed his offspring." (Acts 17:28)

Both quotes are about 'we,' about us. This is so important. Our view of what it means to be human will affect everything about how we live, how we lead others, how we relate to others, how we do singleness or marriage, parenting or childlessness, friendship and work.

Let's ponder the second quote first:

"We are his offspring"

Paul's thinking becomes clear when he goes on to say, 'Being then God's offspring, we ought not to think that the divine being is like gold or silver or stone, an image formed by the art and imagination of man.' (Acts 17:29) He is critiquing their view of the gods, the little statues on their stands. Since we are His offspring, God can't be a little image we come up with. Since we are His

Is God made in our image, or are we made in His?

offspring, who is made in whose image? Is God made in our image, or are we made in His?

Paul's mind was surely thinking back to Genesis 1:26-31. We are made in God's image, not vice versa.

In the first chapter of the Bible we see that humanity made in God's image is the pinnacle of the creation. But what kind of God is He? In the first two verses of Genesis 1 we have God and His Spirit:

> 'In the beginning, God created the heavens and the earth. The earth was without form and void, and darkness was over the face of the deep. And the Spirit of God was hovering over the face of the waters.'

Here is the divine community at the very start. His creation reflects His glorious diversity and generosity. We read of all the plants, fruits, birds, fish and animals. Every leaf is different, every creature unique. There is abundant diversity, yet the wonderful unity of a perfect creation.

The creation account presents a God who is generous and giving, somehow diverse and relational, rather than singular, but without any conflict. As we read on, the Bible reveals a God who is a communicating, speaking, listening, giving, caring, humble, relating God. At His core, God is profoundly relational.

Out of that divine conversation comes a humanity created in His image. 'Let us make man in our image.' The 'us' speaks of conversation, a relational God. So what does it mean to be made in His image? Does it mean we are great abstract thinkers? No hint of that in the text. Does it mean we rule with an iron fist? Again, look closely. (Notice that the tone of the 'dominion' language is not corrupted by power as it has been since the subsequent Fall of humanity.) No, the image of God is not focused on pure rationality or pure power, but is profoundly relational; it is an image that

The image of God is profoundly relational

delights in the other. The divine image-bearers are to rule over creation, and at that point in time, every gazelle and trout and sparrow would have been delighted at the arrangement – ruled

by those made in the image of such a good God! Wonderful!

Those image-bearers are created with inbuilt diversity: male and female. They were significantly different, but genuinely equal. The image of God is found in every individual because we are all relational, but there is something profoundly beautiful about the man and wife as a picture of God's image. Untainted by sin and self-protective competition, a husband and wife would give a glorious presentation of God's nature; working together in harmony and mutual submission to bring forth order and creativity.

Those image-bearers are to be procreative and life-giving, reflecting the nature of God. There would be diversity in each child, but still a unity of family. In chapter 2 we get further detail. You will notice in these first two chapters that everything was good, very good. But in 2:18, something is not good. It is not good for man to be alone. One man made in the image of God was ruling over everything, but his solitude was not good. Why? Because a solo Adam would not be able to effectively represent a God who is a relater.

So God fashioned Eve and brought her to Adam. Adam's response to Eve was typical of grooms looking down the aisle: upon seeing her, the gardener went all poetic! After all the factual presentation and detail of chapters 1 and 2, the climax is profoundly poetic. 'Bone of my bones, flesh of my flesh…' he almost couldn't find the words for this delightful creature before him!

Upon seeing her, the gardener went all poetic!

On my first day at Bible school we were looking at this passage. The professor suggested that understanding the Hebrew is critical at this point. After all, what Adam said of Eve is the climax of the passage. So we all grabbed our pens and got ready for our first ever lesson in Hebrew. He continued, 'When Adam saw Eve, his response was, in the original language… yabba-dabba-doo!!' Not quite Hebrew, but that captured the essence!

This is the climax of Genesis 1 and 2 because this is the image of God. We are not power-mongers, we are not primarily creator-owners, we are relaters made in the image of a God who is a relater. If you start into a conversation with the Father about how great and powerful He is, He would direct your thoughts to His beloved Son who delights Him. And if you speak to the Son and pile on the praise, what would He say? 'My Father is greater than I, I only do what He tells me to do,' etc. The Father points us to the Son and the Son points us to the Father and that is the kind of glory-giving, selfless God that the Bible reveals to us!

This is the kind of glory-giving, selfless God that the Bible reveals to us!

What would Adam have done before the Fall? He would have pointed anyone he met to the wonder of his wife. He was captured and capti-vated and speaking in poetry! To be made in the image of God is not about being self-directed in-dividuals determining our own paths to success. We are made to respond and to relate.

As we read the rest of the Bible we see people living out what it means to dwell either in the reality of God's design and intent, or in the reality of a fallen, me-first, world.

So back to Acts 17, and Paul speaking to philosophers in a post-Fall world. What kind of a God would God be if He were made in our image?

1. A CV WORLD

We live in a world where being human is defined by what you know, what you do, and what you own. That was not God's design. If God were made in our image, we would end up with a God defined by His Curriculum Vitae, His resume. A CV is about distinguishing yourself from others in order to grab attention. If we project this CV mentality on to God, we end up with a god who is all about grabbing attention and trying to make clear that He knows more, can do more, and owns more than anyone else. This version of God fits with philosophical speculation, but also, sadly, it fits with the view of God in many churches that have been deeply marked by this projection of our own ego on to our theology (always with verses attached).

> *For too long we have treated God as a set of facts*

Just because someone knows your CV doesn't mean that they know you. They may know some facts about you, but they don't know you. For too long we have treated God as a set of facts. We may know about Him, but do we know Him? Even if the truths on God's CV are true truths, it doesn't mean we know Him, or what it means to be made in His image.

How easily we project the CV mentality on to God and then live in the light of the image we have created. I need to know more, do more, achieve more, because the more significant I am, the higher my position, the greater my influence, the more distinguished I can be, then the more like God I am and... Voila! The world is introduced to another mini-god!

This approach to life is ugly. It is just as ugly in the church as it is in the world. It comes from a wrong view of God and a wrong understanding of what it means to be made in His image.

Is there a better image we can use? What if we replace the CV with the family portrait?

2. *Life Measured by the Family Portrait*

A CV says 'here are the facts, here is how I am distinguished,' but a family portrait says 'here are the people I am connected to; here are my relationships.' You can do everything to achieve the ultimate CV, but doing so at the expense of family or friendship will always prove to be empty. The fifty-year-old executive who becomes the CEO with a massive salary, but 'celebrates' at an empty kitchen table with a bottle of wine or whisky, trying to numb their loneliness, is a sad advert for CV humanity.

The richness of life comes from relationships. People from many Asian cultures are surprised to learn that in the West our first question on meeting someone new is typically 'What do you do?' They want to know 'Who is your family?' Your place in society, to them, is not defined by what you do, but by who you 'belong' to. God invites us to life defined by relationship because that reflects His nature. He is more concerned about your knowing His Son than about your knowing how much He knows.

The richness of life comes from relationships

So back to Acts 17, and the first quote:

> "In him we live and move and have our being."

Paul was not affirming the intent of the poet with this quote. The poet's meaning, in line with a popular philosophical understanding of the divine at the time, was that since God is everywhere, He is really close: in this table and in this chair and in this wall, etc. So, people believed that the divine being was the ultimate resource in which we live, kind of like saying that the universe itself is divine – that is still CV thinking.

It is in him that we live

Instead, Paul fills the quote with new meaning. In the verses surrounding it, Paul says that it is in Him that we live. It is in relationship to Him, that's what it is to be alive. See verses 26-27:

> 'And he made from one man every nation of mankind to live on all the face of the earth, having determined allotted periods and the boundaries of their dwelling place, that they should seek God, and perhaps feel their way toward him and find him.'

God has providentially orchestrated all the details of history. Why? So that people would seek Him and perhaps reach out for Him and find Him. In verse 30, after debunking the idea that God could be made out of earthly resources, in our image, Paul teaches that God has overlooked such ignorance, but now commands people everywhere to repent.

Repent is such a critical word. It means to turn 180 degrees and go the other way. So what is God commanding people to repent of? Bad behaviour? What is He urging people to turn to? Doing good? That is not what Paul is talking about here (or anywhere else in Acts). Paul is speaking about making God in our own image and doing life our way. He is saying repent of treating God and human life as if it is an exercise in building a CV. Stop trying to be significant, and instead, turn 180 degrees to a God who wants you to be in His family. That is repentance.

Turn to a God who has His arms outstretched to welcome you into His embrace

Turn from living out of wrong values and a wrong view of what it is to be human, and turn to a God who has His arms outstretched to welcome you into His embrace.

He wants us to seek Him and find Him.

Paul was not on some sort of moral crusade to clean up the ancient world; he was preaching about Jesus and the resurrection. He was preaching the gospel. The gospel isn't a command to, 'Behave!' The gospel is a call to be embraced by a loving God who forgives our sin because of Jesus' death. He welcomes us into

The gospel isn't 'Behave!'

His family based purely on our trust in Him. And this gospel brings far more radical moral change than any moral crusade could ever achieve.

Whether we are living a rebellious, sin CV, or a self-righteous, good CV, Paul is preaching that neither is acceptable; we should turn to the God who wants us to find Him.

Life is not about CVs. Life is not about what you know, what you do, what you achieve and what you own. Life is not about how much position you can get, or how much influence you can have, or how much people look to you. Life is not about what, it is about who.

Life is about being in relationship with a God who designed us in His image to enjoy relationship with Him. We are designed to love Him, because He loved us first. That is the gospel. That is what Jesus came to achieve, to call us all to repent from the god of the CV, made in our image, and to come back to the God in whose image we are made. Every time we feel empty in our loneliness, every time we feel hurt in a broken relationship, every time we feel let down when someone treats us as if we were inferior… Paul urges us to come to a God who has created us in His image, who has made the world so we can seek Him and find Him because of what Jesus has done.

Life isn't about what we know, or what we do, or what we achieve, or even about what we own. Life is about who we know, who we love. Do we love ourselves, or the relational God who loved us first?

REFLECTION QUESTIONS

- ❧ How much of your energy goes into building your 'CV' and how much goes into investing in your 'family portrait' of relationships?

- ❧ What are the greatest joys and hurts you can think of that relate to your 'CV' and to your 'family portrait' – does the 'CV' or the 'family portrait' stir the most intense emotions for you?

- ❧ How would you describe your relationship with God? How would you like it to be different?

3: What is Sin?

We are made in the image of a God who is a relater. His primary concern is not to show off and distinguish Himself, but rather to delight in His beloved Son. We are made for relationship with a relational God. So that brings us to the third question: what is our problem? Why are we, by default, separated from God?

Our instinct from birth is not to reach out and rely on God. Our instinct is to be sinful. Sin explains the separation between us and God, but what is sin?

Everyone thinks they know what sin is. Lying, murder, adultery, stealing. And the solution to it? Repent and do the right thing. Turn 180 degrees and stop the sinning, with some belief thrown in, of course, and you have a solution. Isn't

Christianity basically summed up in this: repent of your sins, believe in Jesus and then do good? This needs some probing. Perhaps our problems are deeper than we realise.

PAUL ON SIN

After Paul's missionary journeys he was arrested in Jerusalem and ended up in a prison cell on the coast of Israel. During his two years there he had three trials that are recorded for us in Acts 24-26. In his final trial, where the governor has called in a local Jewish King, Agrippa, to try to make sense of Paul's situation, Paul retells the story of his own conversion to Christianity.

In Acts 26, from verse 12, Paul tells of how he was on a journey to Damascus when Jesus appeared to him and spoke to him. Paul had been a terrorist on behalf of Judaism, capturing followers of Jesus and threatening the church. Jesus had been prodding Paul, but Paul had been resisting, and finally Jesus appeared to him to really get his attention. In verse 18 Paul explains that Jesus told him he was being sent to the Gentiles:

> 'to open their eyes, so that they may turn from darkness to light and from the power of Satan to God, that they may receive forgiveness of sins and a place among those who are sanctified by faith in me.' (Acts 26:18)

Paul continues,

> 'I was not disobedient to the heavenly vision,
> but declared first to those in Damascus, then
> in Jerusalem and throughout all the region
> of Judea, and also to the Gentiles, that they
> should repent and turn to God, performing
> deeds in keeping with their repentance.'
> (Acts 26:19-20)

Notice the repetition of terms here: turn, repent, repentance, and turn. These are important words all through the book of Acts. In fact, they were key words used by the Old Testament prophets, too. Repent or repentance is used eleven times in Acts, and 'turn' is used nine times in the context of someone converting or the preaching of the gospel. If you consider how these words are being used you will find something interesting: what we have here in Acts 26 is the only hint, in the book of Acts, of a connection between repentance and good behaviour! Every time the word repentance is used in the book of Acts (including in this chapter), repentance is about relationship, not behaviour. So the preachers preach that people should turn from worthless idols, from the sin of rejecting Christ, from the sin of crucifying Christ, and turn to what? No, turn to whom! Turn to God. It is not a behavioural turn to good deeds, but a relational turn, to God.

So why does the world think the church is always talking about behaviour, when the early church in the book of Acts was focused on turning to whom? and not to what?

Here in Acts 26:18-20 we see the one possible exception, where Paul references good deeds: '...they should repent and turn to God, per-forming deeds in keeping with their repentance."'But even here, it is proof of the more critical relational

Repentance is not about behaviour, but about relationship

turn, to God. Repentance is not about turning from bad deeds to good deeds. Acts shows that it is about a turn from a relational problem to a relational solution – to turn from sin and turn to God. So, what is sin?

BACK TO THE BEGINNING – GENESIS 3

After the amazing description of God's abundant goodness in creation, and after the pinnacle of creation, humanity was tasked with lovingly ruling the creation under His loving rule. So what happened? In chapter 3 everything went pear-shaped. Sin entered the story. So what is sin?

In this history-shaping passage we read of a conversation between the Serpent and the woman. The Serpent communicated, by implication, 'I've rebelled, and look at me, I'm alive!' The woman had heard from her husband that she must not eat from a particular tree in the midst of the Garden. Then came the question, 'Did God really say?' That question is still resonating today: whose word are we going to trust? The whole of history is being played out under that great question mark. Will we trust the word of God, or will we trust the word of the Serpent? God said 'you will die,' but the Serpent said, 'no, you won't.'

Whose word are we going to trust?

The Serpent denied the death warning and implied that God was actually holding out on humanity. He offered something on the other side of eating that fruit, namely that, 'you will become like God, knowing good and evil.' Eve should have responded incredulously: 'Hang on, Mr. Snake, I am like God, I was made in His image! God has lovingly given us life in His image and we are happily under His loving rule. I am like God!'

'Hang on, Mr. Snake, I am like God, I was made in His image!'

The Serpent was offering a false view of God, so that even in the offer itself there was a lie. He was suggesting that being under God is to be God's doormat. Why wouldn't Eve want to be out from under His rule and instead be in competition as a mini-god determining what is right for her own sphere of influence? Why wouldn't she prefer to be the centre of her own universe as an independent power-broker just like God? There is a lie even in the lie that was told here. Why? Because God is not like that. He is not self-concerned and grabbing and grasping and self-focused. But the Serpent offered the ultimate lie, and Eve bit.

Which way did she choose to go? Did she choose to be loved by a loving and good God, or to be in competition with Him and become the 'god' of her own universe? Even without the Bible we could look at our own lives and know what happened. No child needs to be taught to become the centre of their own universe.

After all the good, good, good, good, they added simply this: evil.

After all the good, good, good, good, they added simply this: evil. Where they had been naked and unashamed, now they realised they were naked and they were ashamed. They covered themselves with fig leaves and hid themselves in fear of God. They started to blame others and protect themselves from blame. We have been doing this ever since.

Eve was deceived, but her husband went in with his eyes wide open. They were promised God-like status, but they received a discovery of their own inadequacy. What a let-down! Sometime, take a look in the mirror and see how much of a god you really are! I'm not a god, but I try to be. I'm inadequate and it is embarrassing, so I feel I must cover and pretend and fake it. I'll pretend I can handle things. Then comes the competitiveness, the fear, the self-protection. As soon as Adam and Eve sinned, they were immediately ready to give their fig-leaf speech.

Instead of being delighted by our delightful God, instead of knowing and loving His loving rule, instead of serving Him with glad hearts, and representing Him to creation... instead we have become competitors. We are now mini-gods with our whole orientation curved in on ourselves. We have become lovers of self: I'm in charge, I can look after me, I will be the centre of the universe. And what goes with that orientation shift? God, I hate you.

What is sin? It is not the poor performance of taking a fruit. It is actually the relational rebellion of wanting to! When Eve looked at the fruit her heart was stirred and captured. Sin is always birthed in our hearts. We sin because we want to. The heart of the human problem is the human heart.

Sin goes much deeper than poor performance. It is about loving self and rejecting a loving God. So how does sin show in our lives? Sin is not primarily a problem with our moral performance, although immorality may be the fruit of sin. Sin is actually a heart-level issue. So how does sin manifest itself?

The heart of the human problem is the human heart.

THE SIN STORY

Jesus told a powerful story about a man with two sons, in Luke 15. The younger son came to his dad and essentially told him that he wished he were dead already – he asked for his inheritance immediately. Strangely, the dad gave him the inheritance and the son went off and lived out the frivolous emptiness of an entertainment lifestyle. He was all about himself, his own fun and activity and sin... Las Vegas style. He lived the life and ended up in a pig-sty before finally coming to his senses, That is, he recognized that his 'room and board' wages, without any 'board,' were not as good as he could earn back at home with his father as the employer. So he decided to go home and try to get a job. His application speech was in his mind all the way back, because he had a plan. He wanted to get a job, and to be paid, and then when he had money, what would he do? Maybe pay off his shame and try to restore his own pride, or maybe just take off again and live the dream once more.

When he got home he encountered something that totally transformed him. He encountered a father who broke all convention, who ran to him and totally humiliated himself and went to extreme lengths to show the son how much he loved him. No middle-eastern man would hoist the skirts of his robe and run – that was humiliating behaviour! It was the love of the father that transformed that young man so that he couldn't even finish his job application speech. Overwhelmed, gawping like a goldfish, he sat at the party. Dressed in the best robe, with a ring on his finger and shoes on his feet, he sat and tried to take it in.

Then there was the older brother. He had never rebelled and had never gone away. He had stayed home and been a good boy. He had been out in the field, and when he got back he found the party in full swing. He asked a servant what was going on and heard of his brother's return and his father's radical grace toward him. The older brother's face grew dark like thunder. With arms crossed and face flinty, the body language screamed his refusal to enter and take his place at the head table.

The father surprised everyone

So what did the father do? Yet again, he surprised everyone. He had already let the younger brother go, and then kept his heart open toward him, and then run through the village humiliating himself, and then showered his rebellious son with undeserved mercy and grace. And now he headed outside to actually beg his older son to come in. Utter self-inflicted humiliation. Who would do such a thing?

We don't know how the story ends, but we do know these two sons are not as different as we might assume. One lived the sinful life, the other lived a supposedly good life. But they weren't opposites. They both wanted to have their dad be a source of benefits, they both wanted to be employees, they both wanted to be paid, they both wanted to take something and go and party with their friends (one in the far country, the other over a goat grill with his friends around the corner). Neither of them wanted relationship with their father, and apparently neither liked him.

If we are not clear what sin is, then we will make the mistake of thinking that the younger brother was the sinner, but the older brother was good.

With a performance-based view of sin, we tend to assume there is a scale. At one end there is 0 out of 50 – really bad; at the other there is 50 out of 50 – consistently good. We live life on this scale and we can't help but do some comparison. 'I am not as bad as that person.'

How many of the sons were lost? Both were. They were both completely lost. One was lost in the far country like a sheep (see Luke 15:1-7). The other was lost close to home like a coin (see Luke 15:8-10). They were both lost. Why? Because sin is not about performance. If it were, then 'Brother Vegas' would be sinful, but 'Brother Righteous' would be good. But the Bible tells us that both versions, both extremes of the sin scale, are sin, because in both there is a heart-level despising of God.

How many of the sons were lost? Both were.

For some of us the sin within us manifests itself in the fruit of a shameful lifestyle. For others of us, the sin of our hearts is manifested in a different form – the pride-laden fruit of self-righteousness. The two manifestations are like a small soft green apple and a large crunchy red apple. Different colours, different tastes, impressing different people, but they are both apples nonetheless.

You can change the colour, you can dye the roots, but sin is sin is sin.

THE GOOD NEWS FOR US ALL

Until we realise that the self-righteous good-performance kind of living is still an act of rebellion against God, we are really going to struggle to explain the Gospel to others (and we will struggle to grasp it for ourselves!). Many of us are 'good' people. We don't steal, we do pay taxes, we may even go to church and give to charity. But if it is me, myself, and I, trying to do the right thing so that I don't get judged, then it is just the fruit of sinful pride coming out in a different way. You can change the colour, you can dye the roots, but sin is sin is sin.

God doesn't save us from a rebellious lifestyle in order to move us into a self-righteous lifestyle. How often have we heard that even if you get 49 out of 50, you still fall short of the glory of God? The truth of the matter is that none of us is at 49. We are all at 0. It could be the soft green apple version of zero, or it could be the crunchy red apple version of zero, but it is zero either way. We may not be as bad as we could be, but in ourselves there is nothing good.

If we are the centre of our own universe and we love ourselves and essentially despise God, then it doesn't matter whether we wear a baseball cap on backwards or wear a tie, it makes no difference, we are still at zero out of fifty.

Maybe you have heard the illustration of a white sheet of paper. If the standard is perfection, then what does it take to be disqualified 'from God's heaven'? Just a single dot of ink. But the truth is that none of us are one-ink-dot people, we are all completely splurged with ink. Some with rebel ink,

It is not just that we are not good enough. It is that we are not good at all!

some with self-righteous ink. Many, like me, are marred with a blended splodge of both.

No-one is righteous, unless we are brought into relationship with God. Righteousness is only to be found in being rescued from the rebellion of setting ourselves up as gods and accepting His welcome back into the relationship He designed us to know.

This is bad news. It is not just that we are not good enough. It is that we are not good at all!

We are in big trouble, if it depends on us. But there is hope. The One represented by the father in the story is One who will go to both the rebellious and the religious in order to humiliate Himself, paying the price for all their multi-coloured sin, to woo them back into relationship with Him. If that is what God is like, if God is self-giving, and if God is willing to humiliate Himself, and if God understands that we are heart-driven responders made in His relational image, and if God will come into this world to rescue us in the most naked, shameful, self-humiliating way possible, then there is hope for sinners like younger Brother Vegas, and hope for older Brother Righteous, and there is hope for a sinner like you, and there is hope for a sinner like me.

The problem is much deeper than we ever imagined, but our final chapter will show how the good news is so much better than we have even dared to dream!

REFLECTION QUESTIONS

🙠 Has your sinfulness tended to manifest itself like the rebellious younger brother, or more like the self-righteous older brother?

🙠 When you consider the extent of the sin in your life, how does it make you feel about a God who would humiliate Himself through death on a cross to save you and bring you into His family?

4: What is Salvation?

At best, many people only have a half-view of sin. They tend to think only of 'sins', and then only superficially. But as we have seen, sin is not simply a matter of how we perform, it goes to the very core of who we are. The heart of the human problem is the human heart. Our hearts are curved in on themselves and consequently we love ourselves and despise God. The outflow of a sinful heart can be a real spectrum of sin. On the one hand the heart spews forth the gross, the immoral, the shameful (Mark 7). But on the other hand you have the respectable, self-righteous, religious, independent sin that is caught up

Our hearts are curved in on themselves

with impressing others while still shaking
the fist at heaven and at God saying, 'I can be
godlike.' Whether it is in self-indulgence or
self-sufficiency, either way, the heart is rebelling
against God.

So the problem facing humanity is much
deeper than we have probably ever realised.
Which means the pressure is on for this chapter,
because if that is the depth of our problem, then
the solution has to be wonderfully good.

If the third foundation stone is the reality
of sin, then the fourth is the grace of God: the
solution to the sin problem. So how good is God's
grace? Is it enough?

THE PROBLEM SUMMARIZED

We have all sinned and fallen short of God's legal
standard. Consequently we are all guilty. Legally
speaking, we are in massive trouble. Our guilt
has to be dealt with by the gospel, otherwise we
are without hope.

But sin is about more than just guilt. Sin
is not just a legal issue. It isn't just about our
criminal record before God. Sin is also about our
relationship with God. It is as if we are in the
dock before the judge, guilty of a crime, but we
are also God's children who are estranged from
Him. We need the penalty for our guilt to be paid,

but we also need to be reconciled to our father. Consequently, while God's grace has to address the need for forgiveness, it also must address the need for friendship. We need a solution to the legal problem of guilt and also the relational problem of separation from God.

If God's grace is going to deal with the relational separation, then it must address the problem of our dead and selfish hearts. Furthermore, it needs to address the great lack in our hearts – the absence of the Holy Spirit. Adam and Eve were created to be united in relationship to each other and to God, and the Spirit of God was the relational glue. The Spirit is the One who communicates the love of the Father to the Son, and the response of the Son to the Father. It is the Spirit who communicated the love of God to Adam and Eve, and carried back the response of their hearts to God. And it was the Spirit who united Adam and Eve in their marital union.

What happened on the day they ate of the fruit? They died. That is, the Spirit departed and from that point on humanity had lost the captivated sense of God's beautiful holiness, the selfless delight in the other person was gone, and they curved in on themselves. They discovered their nakedness and were ashamed of their inadequacy. They started to defend themselves and blame others, fig-leafing their way through what was left of their physical lives. And that was all due to the loss of the Spirit.

Remember how Jesus told Nicodemus that if he wanted to talk about things relating to God, then he would need to be born again, from above, born of the Spirit (John 3:1-15)? Without God's grace we are dead in sin. It is not just a problem of inadequacy. It is a problem of spiritual death because we do not, naturally, have the Spirit of God giving us life. The lack of the Spirit is a critical feature when we think about sin.

So that is our problem: legal guilt, dead hearts and the absence of God's Spirit.

So that is our problem: legal guilt, dead hearts and the absence of God's Spirit.

Grace has to address all of this: both our legal standing, and our relational need. If God's grace only addresses the guilt, then the onus will be on us to perform well and try to win back the lost relationship. But if grace covers it all, if grace is enough, then we have truly good news!

GOOD NEWS WORTH GUARDING

Let's go to Acts chapter 15, where we find the gospel under attack.

Some men were teaching that people had to obey the Law in order to be saved, so Paul and Barnabas were sent up to Jerusalem to the first church council. There they encountered some believers who were from the party of the Pharisees – you can guess where their tendencies might take them. In fact, this was a key moment in the history of the church. Which way would the apostles decide to take the church? Would they agree with the PBBs (Pharisee Background Believers) and affirm that people need to get in God's family properly, via circumcision? Would they agree that in order to stay in God's family and grow properly, people need to keep the Law?

This was a key moment in the history of the church.

This was a gathering of the biggest apostolic names to ponder this question: Is God's grace enough?

If our focus is only on the guilt problem, and we don't grasp the importance of the relational problem, then we will worry that a grace-focus will be totally open to abuse. And it will. If grace only takes care of a guilty record, then the person released will be free to go and sin with abandon. The logic is clear – if you just preach grace then people will sin, and they need to be told how to live, so we must add pressure. If grace only deals with guilt, then the Pharisee Background Believers were right. But God's grace is more powerful than they realised.

Here's how some of the apostles approached the issue:

1. Peter – The Jerusalem Council was convened to avert total disaster in the early church. When Peter stood and spoke to the gathered dignitaries he focused on the giving of the Holy Spirit who purifies the hearts of God's people. Peter then sternly rebuked the notion of adding law to grace. God knows the heart and purifies it by faith through the gift of the Holy Spirit, Peter explained. Notice where Peter focused when he spoke of God's grace in action: on the work of grace that the Pharisees didn't know about. They

> *Grace doesn't just deal with the record; it also establishes the relationship.*

were focused on guilt and protecting people from themselves. However, Peter pointed to God's work of purifying and transforming the hearts of people who simply trust in Him. Grace doesn't just deal with the record; it also establishes the relationship.

God's grace brings people into an intimate relationship with Him so that their hearts actually want to please Him. Grace means the Spirit of God is back, pouring out the love of God into our hearts, and then communicating the cry of our hearts back to God. The Spirit is the key to the transformation of a life so that it will sing out God's righteousness and holiness in a way that duty built on forgiveness alone never can. This is why

God's grace is enough. It does truly transform a life.

Christians can be filled with joy instead of being perpetually sour. Praise God that Peter stood up and said what he said.

2. Barnabas & Paul – Then the whole assembly listened to Barnabas and Paul telling the stories of their ministry among the Gentiles. Can you imagine them taking turns to tell what God had done on Cyprus, or in Pisidian Antioch, or in Lystra, or Derbe? They told story after story of lives transformed from the inside out as the grace of God was preached as the solution to the problem of sin. The whole place fell silent because these two had been on the front lines and they had evidence to support their view that God's grace is enough. It does truly transform a life.

3. *James* – When they finally finished, James spoke up, and the presentation was unanimous. This was James, the half-brother of Jesus. He was one of the family of Jesus that didn't believe in Him. He didn't believe, that is, until he met the risen Christ. If anyone is going to be a reliable witness as to whether Jesus was really back from the dead, surely it is someone who grew up with Jesus and had no vested interest in going along with some sort of resurrection ruse. But James met the risen Jesus and ended up as one of the senior leadership team in the church at Jerusalem.

James spoke with the authority of a teacher, pulling together what Peter had said with what the prophets had taught. Then in verse 19 he gave his position: 'It is my judgment, therefore, that we should not make it difficult for the Gentiles who are turning to God.' (NIV) He suggested that they write a letter and summarize how much of the Law the Gentiles need to be concerned with. Imagine a big digital counter on the wall as James gives his thinking – according to the Jews there were 613 laws. Then the numbers start ticking down: 500, 400, 300, 200, 100… and it finally stops at…4! From 613 down to 4! What a change!

Why was James so lax about the Law? Was he somehow in favour of people diving headlong into libertine licentiousness? Not at all. James knew that if people have got the Spirit and therefore love God and love others, then they will fulfill the Law, so that was not his concern. He was not saying, 'Go and sin!' but, 'They don't need the pressure!'

The four items listed by James might seem confusing, but they make sense in the historical context: Don't eat food offered to idols – this was a real issue in Gentile cultures that could pose a genuine challenge for the Jewish background believers and the Jews who might still be reached; don't commit sexual immorality – this was another common feature of Gentile society, but not fitting for God's people, so let's be alert to that; abstain from strangled animals and from blood – if we want to reach the dispersed Jews then we need to be sensitive. James' concern was not primarily the Gentiles' godliness; it was concern for reaching the Jews. James knew that God's grace establishes a true godliness.

DEFENDING THE GOSPEL OF GRACE

The letter from the Jerusalem council was not the first letter sent to guard the Gospel. Earlier Paul and Barnabas had been followed around Turkey by false teachers who tried to build on what the apostles had taught. 'All this grace, grace, grace emphasis is fine, as far as it goes. It is a good start, but what you really need is to get circumcised – that way you will be properly born again, not just born a bit. And if you are going to take godliness seriously, then you need to live with your eyes on the Law. Get in properly and then go on properly. That is what it means to be truly godly!'

Paul responded to that kind of teaching with his angriest letter, the epistle to the Galatians. Why was he so angry? Because the issue was so important. To turn from the gospel of the grace of God in Christ to the Law is to turn away from the One who called them – i.e. from God Himself (see Gal.1:6). To turn back to the Old Covenant was to turn away from God's provision in the New Covenant!

The grace of God forgives our guilty record, and gives us a new heart.

If the gospel is compromised, it becomes no gospel at all. The grace of God does not simply deal with guilt by forgiving us – amazing as that would be. As well as the clean record, there is also the restored relationship. As well as the forgiveness, there is also the friendship. The grace of God forgives our guilty record, and gives us a new heart – transforming unresponsive, stony, self-concerned hearts to living, feeling, beating hearts that respond to God's self-giving love, so that we want to do what is pleasing to Him. And we are given the grace of God who is the Spirit Himself. So from the closeness of a tight relationship with God we can, from the heart, cry 'Abba!' (Daddy!), because the Spirit is dwelling within and we are united to Christ.

We have heard from Peter, Paul, Barnabas and James. What was the conclusion of the council, and Paul's letter to the Galatians? Is God's grace enough? Yes it is!

GOD'S GRACE REALLY IS GOOD NEWS!

For the past two thousand years, the tendency of the church has always been to suggest that God's grace is not really enough. This is the fleshly tendency of human religion. We may believe that grace is good enough to forgive us, but then typically we feel called to strive and feel the pressure to perform by our own initiative.

Do not misunderstand what is being suggested here. Peter, Paul, Barnabas and James all lived lives marked by godly holiness, by purposeful effort in life and ministry, and by suffering and even martyrdom. They were not advocating a passive and comfortable life of ease. But they were ready to defend God's grace as being sufficient for salvation and transformation.

The grace of God forgives our guilty record, and by the presence of the Spirit, God's grace transforms stony hearts, uniting them to Christ and giving a new desire to do what is right. We don't manufacture that desire to do what is right, nor is the fruit of that desire produced by self-generated effort, but the grace of God will show itself in our lives – from a changed heart will come genuine holiness, purposeful and disciplined godliness, and a self-forgetful willingness to suffer for the sake of God and others.

What happens when grace is not allowed to do its work? We end up with communities of competitive and bitter people, in-fighting and back-biting, power struggles and all the hypocrisy the world is so quick to spot among Christians.

God's provision for the great sin problem is an even greater solution than we could dare to dream. Not only does He wipe away our guilty legal record by His forgiveness, but He also transforms us from the inside out.

The church is the body of Christ in this world. At the centre of the church is the gospel. Around the gospel is the church community, a local church culture that should be permeable

We live in a society where people think Christianity is all about rules

– reflecting the gospel to a watching world so that people are drawn in by the community. The gospel should spill outwards and flow outwards so that lives are transformed. But when we lose sight of the grace of God we put grace in a box and build walls around it: wall after wall after wall, so that people only see us and they don't see grace, because they only see what we are against and not what we are for. We live in a society where people think Christianity is all about rules. How often are Christians asked, 'Hey, does your church allow you to…?' People should look at believers and say, 'I have never seen anyone as alive as you are! Tell me why!'

If the grace of God in the person of the risen Christ was the focus of the church today as it was for the early apostles, how much more would the church be a transformative influence in society!

Sin is far worse than we have ever realised. God's grace is much better than we have ever dared to imagine!

REFLECTION QUESTIONS

- How long would your sin record be before God? Do you believe that the whole record is wiped clean by God's forgiveness?

- How does it make you feel to ponder the relational reality of the gospel? Not only is your record wiped clean, but your relationship with God is restored by the Spirit's work in your heart. Perhaps it would be a good time to tell God how you feel about that.

Part 2

Building on the Four Questions

5: Christian Life & Growth

One more question needs answering before we wrap up the book. Do we get on the same way we got in? That is to ask, is living the Christian life the same package as the gospel by which we get saved in the first place? Many believers act as though it is completely different. They assume we are saved by grace, but we continue by our own efforts, our own learning, and our own diligence.

Let's briefly dip back into Acts again, at the beginning and at the end of Paul's missionary journeys:

AT THE BEGINNING OF THE JOURNEYS: INSTRUCTION FOR NEW BELIEVERS

In Acts 13 we find Paul in Pisidian Antioch (located in what is now called Turkey). He preaches a biblically saturated sermon in a Jewish synagogue, urging the listeners to trust in the risen Christ for forgiveness of sins and justification. He warns them not to reject the message, and the writer describes Paul and Barnabas urging the new believers to 'continue in the grace of God.'

So the grace of God was the emphasis, referring to the forgiveness of sins and being made right with God. The focus is on their guilt being dealt with because of Jesus' death and resurrection. Simple trust in His work at Calvary makes it possible to be legally justified: to have a clear conscience and a record wiped clean. We have pondered this in the previous chapter. Satan may bring up memories and guilt, but if we are recipients of God's grace, then we are free.

> *My sin, O the bliss, of this glorious thought,*
> *My sin, not in part, but the whole,*
> *Is nailed to the cross and I bear it no more,*
> *Praise the Lord, praise the Lord, O my soul!*

Our 'criminal record' before God is a serious issue, but it can be wiped clean by the grace of God. What about the rest of the problem? Does this passage only point to the legal, but not the relational problem? Does it offer pardon, but no power for living?

Acts 13 goes on to describe Paul's return to the synagogue the following week and concludes with a summary, starting in verse 49. The word of the Lord spread through the whole region but, as was typical, the reaction of the non-responsive religious folk drove Paul and Barnabas away. But the story ends with this: 'And the disciples were filled with joy and with the Holy Spirit.'

This is the fruit of the grace of God at work. It was not merely legal, as amazing as that would be. It was relational. If the gospel were merely a legal change of status, then the Christian life would be characterized mainly by diligence and responsibility. But actually the gospel changes our status, and also does much more!

The gospel changes our status, and also does much more!

These people who had been dead in their hearts were now filled with the Holy Spirit and their hearts were alive to God in joy. There is the legal, but also the relational; the forgiveness, but also the friendship. That is the grace of God – it is big enough to deal with the whole problem.

To put it simply, this means that the Christian life is not about our own responsible effort to live up to our new status. The Christian life is a relationship with God, by His Spirit. He works in our hearts and we grow in our love for Him and for others. Love is not something we work up by determination; it is a response to Christ as He is revealed more and more to our hearts by the Spirit. So we need to live our lives in the same way we received life in the first place – by fixing the gaze of our hearts on Christ and living in response to Him. This is what it means to be filled with joy and with the Holy Spirit. This is what it means to continue in the grace of God.

> *We need to live our lives in the same way we received life in the first place – by fixing the gaze of our hearts on Christ*

AT THE END OF THE MISSIONARY JOURNEYS:
INSTRUCTION FOR ESTABLISHED CHURCH LEADERS

As we read on through Acts we find that Paul's three missionary journeys are followed by his arrest and trials. As Paul headed to Jerusalem after the third journey, he knew trouble was brewing. He had collected an offering from Gentile churches and was travelling back to Jerusalem to present it to the Jewish background believers.

For Paul, the unity of the 'mother church' in Jerusalem with the new churches across the region was really critical. In fact, the health of the church was more important to him than his own well-being. So he journeyed on with the gift and a group of representatives who were handling the money on behalf of their home churches. He knew he was heading for trouble.

As Paul traveled toward Jerusalem, he took the opportunity to connect with the elders from Ephesus. He knew that if he headed into the city of Ephesus itself, he would get stuck there, as he had many friends in the region. So he had a quick rendezvous with the elders at a place called Miletus, on the coast, and then pressed on toward Jerusalem in order to arrive by the feast of Pentecost. In Acts 20 we read Paul's speech to these dear elders. His speech was a fond farewell, a heartfelt encouragement to stay true to what they had received, and to guard the church under their care.

Paul reflected on his ministry in their region, how he had served God with 'all humility and with tears and with trials' – which were problems brought against him by the non-responsive religious folks. He had confidently preached to them all, both to Jews and to non-Jews, about repentance towards God and faith in Christ. Notice, as we saw before, that in Acts, repentance and faith are not a call to turn from bad behaviour to good

Paul's message was a call to a relationship.

behaviour, combined with assent to some key theological facts. Rather, Paul's message was consistently one of turning to God and trusting in the Lord Jesus Christ. Paul's message was a call to a relationship.

Paul then focused on what was coming next for him as he continued his journey:

> 'And now, behold, I am going to Jerusalem, constrained by the Spirit, not knowing what will happen to me there, except that the Holy Spirit testifies to me in every city that imprisonment and afflictions await me. But I do not account my life of any value nor as precious to myself, if only I may finish my course and the ministry that I received from the Lord Jesus, to testify to the gospel of the grace of God.' (Acts 20:22-24)

Paul was living a life responsive to the Holy Spirit at work in him. He was ready to lay down his own life for the sake of this message – the gospel, the good news, of the grace of God.

As Paul comes to the end of his heartfelt speech, he tells them that they won't see him again. He is able to look back on his ministry among them with confidence that he had not held back anything from 'the whole counsel of God.' He urged these men to continue his work by caring for and protecting the flock of God's people. What would they need protecting from?

Paul anticipated a two-fold threat to the flock. First, wolves would come in from outside. Second, people from within the church would speak a twisted message that would draw people away after them. Even today the church remains vulnerable on these two counts. In many places, the greater threat is probably not the attacks from outside, but the twisting of the gospel from inside.

So how did Paul summarize the message these elders were to guard in the days ahead?

Even today the church remains vulnerable on these two counts.

> 'And now I commend you to God and to the word of his grace, which is able to build you up and to give you the inheritance among all those who are sanctified.' (Acts 20:32)

With these words, Paul was not reducing the gospel, or saying that ministry does not require effort. Ministry does take significant effort, and in Paul's last words (vv. 33-35) he went on to describe the hard work of giving ourselves and our ministry to others. But don't miss the impact of his description of the ministry itself. It is about the word of God's grace – 'which is able to build you up and to give you the inheritance among all those who are sanctified.' It is the message of God's grace that builds up a group of believers and establishes them fully among the wider community of those who have been set apart by God's work in their lives.

Here is a critical point for us to end this little survey of Paul's ministry in Acts ... we will grow up in Christ the same way we got in . It is God's grace that saves us, and it is God's grace that builds us up and changes us into His transformed people.

REFLECTION QUESTIONS

-   How often does your gaze slip from Christ to yourself when it comes to living the Christian life?

-   Imagine being the bride in the first dance with Christ as the groom – what will that dance be like if you focus on yourself and try hard to dance well, as opposed to fixing your gaze on Him and responding to His lead?

6: The Four Questions Applied

In this little book we have been listening to Paul's words as recorded in the book of Acts. In many ways we have barely scratched the surface of Acts, and we have not dived into the richness of Paul's thirteen New Testament letters from Romans to Philemon. Let me encourage you to take on that adventure for yourself. Read through the whole of Acts and keep going into Paul's letters. As you read, keep asking the four great questions that form the foundation of our beliefs – Which God? What does it mean to be human? What is sin? What is the solution / salvation?

And when you finish Paul's letters, why not keep going to the end, and then start all over again from Genesis? The Bible can seem like a daunting collection of ancient documents, but reading it through at a pace can become the greatest source of delight in your life. Instead of trying to grasp every detail, look for the answers to the four questions. Get to know God as He reveals Himself through the Bible, and discover what it means to live in relationship with Him.

Reading the Bible can become the greatest source of delight in your life!

In this last chapter I want to call us to keep these four questions front and centre in three areas of our Christianity – in our personal relationship with Christ, in our evangelism, and in our church ministries.

THE FOUR QUESTIONS AND YOU

When the gospel of God's grace in Jesus Christ grips a life, amazing things happen. That person goes from living as a mini-god at the centre of their own universe to being a child of the true God, a friend of God, and a member of the collective bride of Christ. Legally their status is changed from guilty to righteous. Internally their desires which were solely self-directed become captured by Christ. They start to want to know

Him more and to please Him. Spiritually they go from being dead toward God, to having the Spirit of God living in them and stirring them with a new appetite for Christ. All that, and more, occurs in the instant that they respond to the loving invitation of the gospel to trust Christ for life.

I hope that last paragraph resonates with you. If you find yourself feeling like it doesn't describe you, but you want it to, then maybe this is the moment where God's Spirit is drawing you to turn from your version of sinful living and turn to God. Maybe this is the moment when He is prompting you to trust in the person of Christ and His death on the cross to make full payment for your sin. Maybe this is the moment to invite the risen Christ to bring the gift of life to you.

There is a spiritual gravity in this world that will always pull us away from the wonder of the gospel

Whether you just believed or have been a follower of Jesus for many years, you need to keep the four questions front and centre in your life. Why? Because there is a spiritual gravity in this world that will always pull us away from the wonder of the gospel. Let me explain.

We looked briefly at Genesis 3 back in the third chapter (the chapter on sin). When sin entered our world it corrupted everything. Everything. And yet we have grown up in a fallen world convinced that what is normal, is just that, normal. It isn't. Everything is upside-down and inside-out, but naturally we just can't see that. So when we trust in Christ we have new and unique access to truth, but we still live in a fallen world. And the gravity of this world, and our own flesh, will continue to pull us away from the wonder of the gospel and down into a reduced version of what God wants for us.

God? Our view of God will naturally fall from the wonder of being offered relationship with the Trinity (the Father-Son-Spirit God) into a more distant and cold version of God. The fallen world elevates the notion of a power-hungry god out to devour and demand. The Bible tells us that this is a description of the 'god of this age,' (see 1 Peter 5:8 for instance, where our enemy is described as a roaring lion eager to devour). It is scary how we can so easily assign devilish descriptions to the true God and end up with a more distant arrangement between Him and us. We diminish Him into a glory-hungry law-giver –

distant and focused merely on the legal matters. When that happens, our relationship with God suffers.

Human? Our view of humanity will easily slide back towards the myth of selfish independence, and this easily continues even as believers in Christ. How? Well, the Bible repeatedly teaches us that we are heart-centred and responsive beings. It teaches us that we are defined by our relationships, by who or what we love, rather than by our self-determined achievements – what we know, do, or own. But the world drip-feeds the autonomous view. Almost every message coming to us today comes with a silent hiss from Genesis 3 that we would do well to detect. If we don't keep the question of what it means to be human front and centre, then we can easily start trying to do a churchy version of what the world does: a Christian version of diligent effort and personal discipline. This may sound spiritual, but it can so easily lapse into an independent striving for identity and spiritual development. We are

> *We are made in the image of a relational God for a life defined by healthy relationships*

made in the image of a relational God for a life defined by healthy relationships with one another, and primarily, with God Himself!

Sin? Our view of sin will always be way too small when our thinking is shaped by a fallen impulse, rather than by the washing with water of the Word of God. We will tend to think of sin as merely bad behaviour. Sin becomes something we do. Actually, something other people do. We all have an infinite capacity, as fallen creatures, to rationalize and ignore any sin that is visible in the mirror, while condemning any sin we see in others. However, as we keep the 'what is sin?' question before us and keep soaking our hearts and minds in the Bible, we will continue to see sin for the heart problem that it is. God will keep revealing more and more of the depths of the sin and corruption in our hearts and we will continue to see how it manifests in our lives, both in 'younger brother rebellion' and in 'older brother religiosity.'

Salvation? Our view of salvation will always slide back into being essentially a legal contract if we don't keep the fourth question before us. That is, we will naturally fall into the idea that a distant and law-obsessed God has offered us some sort of legal loophole offering salvation. Our responsibility is then to demonstrate our commitment in order to get some benefit. Salvation slips into being just a change in our legal status. Our fleshly human nature always wants to earn what we get from God. This will mess with how we view our salvation, and how we seek to mature in our salvation. Remember, the way we get on is the same way we got in – by looking to Christ and responding to Him. It is not a matter of our exercise and effort, but of maintaining our closeness to Christ and growing in that relationship.

If we keep the four questions front and centre, then our relationship with Christ will be enriched and healthy. They will help us to see what the Bible is saying, and most importantly, who it is revealing.

These questions will help us as we pray, live our lives, serve the church, *Most importantly, who is the Bible revealing?* face temptations, make decisions, and grow up into all that God wants for us to be. When these four questions slip out of view, then the 3-dimensional, rich, relational Christianity will subtly morph into a thinner 2-dimensional version, marked by distance from God and concern over personal performance.

THE FOUR QUESTIONS AND EVANGELISM

God? As we looked at Paul's preaching to completely pagan folks in Lystra and Athens, we saw how he was primarily concerned with the first of these four questions. Which god is God? Let us keep that question in view and stop trying to convince people that there is a 'simple God' out there – some sort of all alone, power-driven God. The Bible doesn't call us to convert a culture of atheists into theists, it calls us to abide in Christ, know Him, and then join Him in His mission to make His Father known. The God we can present to the world is an absolute delight.

The greatest joys and the greatest agonies always come in the context of relationships.

Human? Once we get clarity on the first question, then the other three flow from it. Most people sense that there must be more to life than the performance, achievement, ownership and pleasure version of life that the world keeps offering. With the second question in view, we can help people to understand why the greatest joys and the greatest agonies always come in the context of relationships.

Sin? Too many people in our culture have a skewed and thinned version of Christianity in view. Too many gospel presentations have given the impression that God is mean, distant and petty. After all, He sends people to hell for the tiniest infractions – have you ever stolen a paper clip from the office? We need to help people understand that sin goes far deeper than behaviour. Ultimately, God is primarily concerned to transform their self-absorbed hearts.

Salvation? In light of the wonder of our glorious triune God, and the richness of being made in His relational image, and the frighteningly bad news of our own incurred souls, then comes the best news of all. As we keep the four questions in view, we have something so rich to offer – not only legal justification, but also a new heart and a new relationship of union with Christ by the Spirit.

When the four questions drift from our view, fallen world gravity will pull us away from the real wonder of the Gospel. Our evangelism will grow dry and formulaic, and any converts we see will likely be struggling from the very beginning. As we read our Bibles and ponder the four questions, we will be more captivated by the amazing message of the Gospel.

THE FOUR QUESTIONS AND CHURCH

Fallen world gravity doesn't just pull us away from the wonder of the Gospel as individuals, it does the same to our churches. How many denominations and churches have begun with vibrant relational faith and eventually slipped into a form of godliness, but totally bereft of any power? How can we best help our own churches be communities of vibrant spiritual health?

It will not be by means of the latest and greatest seminars, or a bold emphasis on application in preaching, or greater commitment from us or anyone else. Health is wrapped up in the foundations of the Gospel. If we introduce others to the four questions and keep them central in our church life, then health can flourish.

God? We don't worship a generic supreme being. We worship the God of the Bible. As we preach the Bible, let's be sure to put the focus not on what we should do, but on who He is. Let's share with each other, both in formal ministry like preaching, and in informal conversation, about the wonder of who our God is. Everyone needs to be continually introduced to the wonderful God who wants to be known in our churches!

Human? We aren't self-moved commitment machines. We are made in the image of a rela-tional God. Consequently what people need is not mere education to know more, nor peer pressure (or pulpit pressure) to perform better. People need to be offered Christ so that their hearts might be stirred afresh in each season of life so that they might live 'hearty' lives for Jesus. This isn't a call to abandon educational ministries, nor to stop preaching instruction for life. It is a call to recognize that people will do what they want, and we can't control their 'wants.' Instead, what we can do is

We can't control our own hearts

enthusiastically offer the wonder of our glorious Christ to one another so that our churches are vibrant communities of responsive believers, vulnerably facing life together with God's Spirit at work in our midst.

Sin? We are not just people with sin in our past. We still struggle with sin. We will continue to struggle as long as we live in this fallen world, and in bodies that are still hard-wired to pull towards independence from God. Our sin may not manifest itself in the gross behaviours that used to be normal for some of us, but it will show up in more acceptable religious and self-righteous garb. The heart of the human problem is the human heart, and we can't control our own hearts. But God can change them. Let's try to make our churches communities of real people being real with each other about the struggles we face as our personal desires compete within us. Let's look for ways to spur one another on toward love and the resulting good deeds.

Salvation? We aren't people with merely a ticket to heaven. Too many churches are filled with people who have some sort of legal arrangement with God, but no meaningful relationship with Him. We are called to a dynamic relationship with Christ that is by faith now, but someday will be face to face for eternity. The church should be a community gripped by the gospel, not by a prune-juice commitment to sour faces and prickly conduct codes. As we are gripped by the gospel, the wonder of our union with Christ – our forgiveness, our heartfelt desire to know and obey Him, and our fellowship with Him and each other by the Spirit – this will make our church communities compellingly attractive. The world looks at the church and often sees hypocrisy. They see people complaining about the conduct of others while living inconsistently themselves. Let's keep the four questions front and centre so that we become compelling communities of gospel life: delighting in the Trinity, overflowing with love for others, and living out a heartfelt gospel integrity that surpasses anything we can muster by our own efforts.

REFLECTION QUESTIONS

ॐ How can you keep the four questions in your own thinking? How can you promote clarity on these questions and their answers within your church community?

ॐ What impact could the church make in your region if the believers were gripped by the relational richness of the God who is Trinity, of our being made in His image, and the heart-changing wonder of the Gospel?

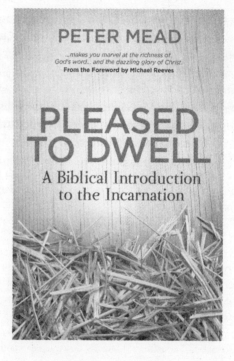

PETER MEAD

...makes you marvel at the richness of
God's word... and the dazzling glory of Christ.
From the Foreword by Michael Reeves

PLEASED TO DWELL

A Biblical Introduction
to the Incarnation

ISBN 978-1-78191-426-7

Pleased to Dwell

A Biblical Introduction to the Incarnation

PETER MEAD

At the centre of heaven is Christ, lovingly adored as the forever Lord of all. At the centre of Christmas is Christ, frail and cradled in the tender arms of a young mother. How can the two be put together? Heavenly glory and human frailty? That is the real wonder of Christmas. *Pleased to Dwell* is an energetic biblical introduction to Christmas. It is an invitation to ponder the Incarnation, and a God who was please to dwell with us.

> What a really useful resource! As I read through it, I found that ideas for carol service talks just kept leaping off its pages.
>
> RICO TICE,
> Author, *Christianity Explored* &
> Associate Minister at All Souls Church, Langham Place, London

> This book is perfect food for the heart for all of us who long for a richer understanding of the birth of The King!
>
> JOSEPH M. STOWELL,
> President, Cornerstone University, Grand Rapids, Michigan

> In this book we see the profound truths of the incarnation presented in a way that makes the Bible and its truth come alive. And, best of all, it is presented in an engaging style that makes it accessible to ordinary laypersons.
>
> AJITH FERNANDO,
> Teaching Director, Youth for Christ, Sri Lanka

Christian Focus Publications

Our mission statement –

STAYING FAITHFUL

In dependence upon God we seek to impact the world through literature faithful to His infallible Word, the Bible. Our aim is to ensure that the Lord Jesus Christ is presented as the only hope to obtain forgiveness of sin, live a useful life and look forward to heaven with Him.

Our books are published in four imprints:

CHRISTIAN
FOCUS

Popular works including biographies, commentaries, basic doctrine and Christian living.

CHRISTIAN
HERITAGE

Books representing some of the best material from the rich heritage of the church.

MENTOR

Books written at a level suitable for Bible College and seminary students, pastors, and other serious readers. The imprint includes commentaries, doctrinal studies, examination of current issues and church history.

CF4•K

Children's books for quality Bible teaching and for all age groups: Sunday school curriculum, puzzle and activity books; personal and family devotional titles, biographies and inspirational stories – Because you are never too young to know Jesus!

Christian Focus Publications Ltd,
Geanies House, Fearn, Ross-shire,
IV20 1TW, Scotland, United Kingdom.
www.christianfocus.com